The Black Bubble

Uriah Brown

ISBN:1519435681
ISBN-13:9781519435682

DEDICATION

I dedicate this book to Iris & Godfrey Brown, two amazing parents who gave their all to ensure I had a better future. Their impressive career as parents advanced my success, inspired me to believe I am capable of writing a book, and speaking when I thought I had no voice. I also dedicate this book to Rukiya Goddard, for you believed in me when no one else did.

CONTENTS

ACKNOWLEDGMENTS

Any work, materials, opinions and findings expressed in this book are from the voices of the African American community. Those constantly denied economic and social justice was given the opportunity to be used as the framework in creating "The Black Bubble." Uriah Brown wishes to thank all the participants who was brave enough to tell their story to the world. Hopefully those too frightened to tell the truth will one day take the stage and be brave enough to speak.
A special acknowledgement to Professor Lloyd Carr for his extensive support.

There are few attempts to improve the quality of life for African Americans. Their experiences are still shaped by institutionalized disadvantages that do not grant them access to equal opportunities in America. I am not the most informed person in the country on Racism and Discrimination, I merely fit the criteria needed to inform people that the issue of Racism and Discrimination is still a significant problem in this country. African Americans have been placed in what I call **"The Black Bubble"**; an institutionalized barrier that creates a barricade to success. It is ironic the people who have played the largest role in the economic development of this country receive no political, economic or social support from it. Because of this legacy of institutionalized disadvantages for some and government enabled advantages for others, the distribution of wealth and power in America is clearly unevenly dispersed. Despite what society may portray, African Americans and White Americans live in racially segregated areas with minimal contact as possible. White areas of course produce and receive much more resources than Black and brown spaces. This book will be a testimony of the disadvantages African Americans face every day, it will critically analyze the way America (land of the free) dehumanizes African Americans so they are never given a fair chance to accumulate wealth, power or know themselves.

Uriah Brown

1.

The educational system so many rely upon is substantially broken. It is rigged so African Americas never have a fair shot at achieving success. With its current design, America deflates the value in Black education because education is largely influenced by the level of income family's hold. According to the article *Black America's Education Crisis:*

> "Achievement gaps between white and black children and between high-poverty and high-income families shows up before children even enter school..... Once they're in school low income children are on average three years behind by the time they reach the fourth grade"(Talbert, Goode 72).[1]

This suggest, the education students receive is relative to their income bracket; if you are poor you will never receive a just and equal education. A partial system will only continuously produce students who are not prepared for the real world and Blacks who cannot read or write on grade level.

We have for too long pretended the conditions ascribed to African Americans are random in practice when in fact they are government enabled. Black students receiving less health care

---

[1]Talbert, Marcia Wade, and Robin White Goode. "Black Americans Education Crisis." Black Enterprise 42.2(2011):71-75.academic search com,plete.web.27 May 2012.

than White students will have more absences in school because they are sick more often. After a history of inadequate education for African Americans, Black families who are less educated and illiterate, will not be able to expose their children to advance vocabulary at home. As these disadvantages persist the likelihood of low income African Americans achieving a just and equitable education are improbable. Most African Americans in public schools are from low income families, and have little or no health insurance. Grouping academically drifting students together creates an unfit learning environment. Think of it this way, if a man works a low income job his entire life, his ability to obtain resources are limited, but if this man somehow obtains the chance to work a middle class job, his quality of life will increase. The same logic applies to education. If you are grouping struggling students with other struggling students, their ability to gain more resources will prove difficult because these students cannot learn from each other. Grouping underachieving students with those who are competing on or above grade level might be enough to help those students excel in their academic work.

During the Brown vs. Board of education trial, the court stated separate educational facilities are inherently unequal, that it was a violation of our civil rights paving the way for what was supposed to be desegregated schools. Instead of racially separating students, students are separated by their income. The irony is, the majority of Black students are from of low income families and because of the wage gap; will never sit in the same classroom and obtain the same classroom resources as Whites.

To exercise unjust power over people requires a substantial level of ignorance and poorly educated citizens. The inadequate education received by African Americans limits the amount of opportunities presented to them, which increases their risk of being poor. Poorly educating African Americans puts the entire American economy at a disadvantage. African Americans account for 13.2% of the American population. If African Americans are not properly prepared for the real world, they will not develop the necessary skills needed to perform the complicated and skilled positions America requires. According to the *Scott Foundation:*
"The total annual economic burden to taxpayers because of educational inequality is $59.2 billion, Closing the achievement gap could have increased 2008 annual gross domestic product by $1.3 trillion to $2.3 trillion"(Talbert, Goode 73).[2]

There are racial biases against predominately Black schools vs. White schools. According to *the Center for American Progress,* predominantly Black schools generally receive less funding and

---

[2]Talbert, Marcia Wade, and Robin White Goode."Black Americans Education Crisis." Black Enterprise 42.2(2011):71-75.academic search com,plete.web.27 May 2012.

their facilities are usually in worse shape than that of their white counter part. They usually have old and outdated textbooks, very little supplies and work conditions are inadequate(73).[3] Because African Americans receive the lowest quality of education, their political and civil rights can constantly be violated. Police officers can regularly harass and assault Black citizens because they have not been taught the rights they have. The media constantly portrays the issue of Black education as if it lives in a vacuum and has no relationship to color, when in fact American education is directly linked to Racism and Discrimination. This country wonders why Black public schools across the nation are failing, when it is because of the inefficient budget these Black institutions receive annually that contributes to these closings. According to the article *Black America's Education Crisis,* the Teacher Federation sued New York City because it was giving out separate funding. The city was giving more money to charter schools, and less money to public schools. Charter schools educate 4% of the city students, and public schools educate the other 96%(75).[4] With the majority of Black students enrolled in public schools, the entire

---

[3]Talbert, Marcia Wade, and Robin White Goode."Black Americans Education Crisis." Black Enterprise 42.2(2011):71-75.academic search com,plete.web.27 May 2012.

[4]Talbert, Marcia Wade, and Robin White Goode."Black Americans Education Crisis." Black Enterprise 42.2(2011):71-75.academic search com,plete.web.27 May 2012.

student body of New York City regularly competes for a fraction of the resources. This devalues and dehumanize education for African Americans.

African and Latin Americans lag behind their White counterparts in the classroom. On average African Americans are more likely to get expelled from school, drop out of high school, and are less likely to enroll or graduate from college. New York and Nebraska are the two states with the highest educational gap, leading with a 43% gap(pg.9).[5] Researchers are conducting experiments to confront the issue of low achieving Black students. They believe that if classrooms for African Americans are single sexed, they could possibly achieve more. But according to *the U.S Department of Education*, academic outcomes in single sex and coeducational classrooms concluded that no positive benefits will arise from single sexed classrooms(10).[6] Some neuroscientist claims African Americans may just have a learning deficiency but research suggests there is no evidence to support that (10).[7] It is almost as if this country will blame anything else for a catastrophe they have been fueling for decades than taking responsibility for

---

[5]Noguera, Pedro A."Saving Black And Latino Boys".Phi Delta Kaplan 93.5 (2012):8-12. Academic Search Complete.web.27 May 2012.

[6]Noguera, Pedro A."Saving Black And Latino Boys".Phi Delta Kaplan 93.5 (2012):8-12. Academic Search Complete.web.27 May 2012.

[7]Noguera, Pedro A."Saving Black And Latino Boys".Phi Delta Kaplan 93.5 (2012):8-12. Academic Search Complete.web.27 May 2012.

the educational crisis they created. Never once will America admit the role Racism plays in the educational stall of African Americans.

To learn efficiently students have to be place in an environment that produces a calm, safe and stable learning atmosphere. Disregarding the fact that this country is racially bias, Whites still are placed in settings that are less hostile, more spacious and has more opportunities. The education process begins before school starts and after it ends. Positive relationships with teachers and providing students with strong professional mentors and counselors can make a difference in student's success. Black and brown schools usually have fewer mentors to provide their students with. How can students excel in environments that are more hostile and dangerous? How can they focus on getting good grades and what they read in their textbooks when they constantly have to look over their shoulders? How can they excel if the system is designed for them to fail?

White Privilege and Racism impacts the entire educational sector. **White Privilege** is an advantage White Americans possess that gives them more opportunities than minorities. **Racism** is a system of disadvantage based on race. An academic environment like college is not exempt from the disadvantages White Privilege and Racism offers to minorities. The entire graduate admissions process is fixed so Whites will always have an advantage over subordinate groups like African Americans and Latinos. The GRE examination is a prime example of inequity in exam assessments. According to Baumgartner and Bailey "they have analyzed that the GRE is a biased exam that creates disadvantages for members of different minority groups and still the GRE is heavily weighted in admissions decisions"(28).[8] How can an exam that creates disadvantages for African Americans and Latinos be the criteria for admissions? The GRE is the criteria for admissions because it gives Whites an edge in education. According to the article *Racism and White Privilege in Adult Education Graduate Programs:* "The vocabulary section of the GRE is culturally biased against international students and those from low socioeconomic backgrounds in that it is normed and developed on English speaking white middle class subjects, whose set of educational experiences generally differ from the experiences of people of color and immigrants"(Baumgartner and Bailey 29).[9] In other

---

[8]Baumgartner,Lisa M., Juanita Johnson-Bailey. "Racism and White privilege in adult education graduate programs: Admisiions, retentions, and curricula". New direction for adult & continuing education125 (2010):27-40.academic search complete.web.28 May 2012.

[9]Baumgartner,Lisa M., Juanita Johnson-Bailey. "Racism and White privilege in adult education graduate programs: Admisiions, retentions, and curricula". New direction for adult & continuing education125 (2010):27-40.academic search complete.web.28 May 2012.

words, African Americans and other minorities who take the GRE examination, will be taking an exam they have never been prepared for or accustomed to. When Whites take the GRE they have a better chance of receiving a higher score because the exam is culturally conditioned to what they have been learning their entire life. When African Americans take the GRE their chances of a high score is lower even if they have studied and entered into study programs because the test does not relate to their educational curriculum. This is another signal that indicates the education Whites and Blacks receive are completely different. It would be fair to say, assessing students educational level on these fraudulent standardized exams are both a waste of time and inefficient. Making life changing decisions as to accept or not accept a student based on their GRE grades are ridiculous, especially when the exam is culturally biased. African Americans are taught one thing, tested on something completely different, and are expected to do well. The fondest thing is that when they do not test well our society then stereotypes African Americans to be less intelligent then Whites, even though Blacks have been cheated out of a fair chance to show their intelligence. According to the article *Racism and White Privilege in Adult Education Graduate Programs:* "A comprehensive survey, administered to over 2000 black students who received graduate degrees from the university of Georgia adult education program between 1962 and 2003 showed that support and social experiences between black and white counter parts were different......black students were subjected to police harassment, isolation in classrooms, and racial epithets"(Baumgartner and Bailey 31-32).[10]

How exactly are African Americans supposed to learn and develop life skills in environments like those? The truth is half of all African Americans in public schools are going to fail. It is a harsh reality, and it is largely because of the psychological impact of Racism.

The psychological impact of Racism is tremendous, and it serves as a massive determinant of the behavior and intellectual potential of Black students. Blacks are burdened with this hardship and have to live life with this enigma following them wherever they go. In retrospect Whites do not carry the burden of Racism in a negative manner, it is held proudly on their shoulders which positively impacts their lives. Not having the burden of Racism follow you wherever you go is a privilege. That is an advantage in life. Having that one less thing to worry about creates a huge advantage in the classroom. While White students are able

---

[10]Baumgartner,Lisa M., Juanita Johnson-Bailey. "Racism and White privilege in adult education graduate programs: Admisiions, retentions, and curricula". New direction for adult & continuing education125 (2010):27-40.academic search complete.web.28 May 2012.

to participate freely in school, Black students are pondering about why they are the constant subject of police harassment. Discriminating against a student because of race can cause that student to believe the stereotypes aimed against him/her creating a self-fulfilling prophecy.

According to the article say it loud, I'm black and I'm proud: **"Racial Socialization**, the process by which parents teach their children about the significance and meaning of race....may counteract negative racist experiences, influence academic motivation, and lead to increased academic performance" (Neblett, Chavous, Nguyen, Sellers 246).[11]

Racial socialization is a tool that can be used to inform African Americans about who they are. Taking that first step is what African Americans must do before they can seek success in America. According to *say it loud I'm black and I'm proud:* even though African Americans do experience Racism, it does not deteriorate them from wanting to learn, it just makes it harder for them to learn (Neblett, Chavous, Nguyen, Sellers 225).[12]

---

[11]Robert M. Sellers,etal."say it loud—I'm black and I'm proud":parents' messages about race, racial discrimination, And academic achievement in African American Boys."Journal of negro education 78.3(2009):246-259. Academic search complete.web.27 May 2012.

[12]Robert M. Sellers,etal."say it loud—I'm black and I'm proud":parents' messages about race, racial discrimination, And academic achievement in African American Boys."Journal of negro education 78.3(2009):246-259. Academic search complete.web.27 May 2012.

Opportunities are rarely presented for individuals from low socioeconomic backgrounds. Children from these backgrounds tend to perform worse in classrooms than individuals from middle class and upper class environments. According to *why our schools are segregated*: "In 1989 black students typically attended schools in which 43 percent of their fellow students were low income; and by 2007 that figure has risen to 59 percent"(Rothstein 51).[13] White children from low socioeconomic backgrounds are less likely to be placed in classrooms with individuals from the same socioeconomic background. They are more likely to be integrated into classes mixed with children from middle class backgrounds. Segregation is not only racial but socioeconomic as well. Black students are pegged to stay with other Black students, while White students are free to room with anyone that will be a potential stepping stone in helping them achieve more in their academic career.

Racial Isolation causes African Americans to bring so much more problems into the classroom. Since they have become social pariahs there is no one available for these students to look up to, nor to offer real socioeconomic support. Imagine having over 8.4 million students all experiencing relatively the same issues both at

---

[13]Rothstein, Richard."why are our schools segregated."Educational Leadership.May2013,Vol.70 Issue 8,p50-55.6p.Academic search complete.

home and economically, add low funding from the state, parents without any real formal education, classmates just as deprived as they are, teachers resistant to help because of laziness, and a government that encourages the segregation of educational resources and you tell me how exactly are we expected to help minorities overcome these challenges? According to Rothstein: "studies confirm that students of different races benefit from working together and are better prepared for civic engagement." (Rothstein 52).[14] Students perform better when they are racially desegregated because Whites tend to have more resources than Blacks, sharing those resources helps everyone. Whites are not naturally smarter than African Americans, but because of this legacy of unequal distribution of resources, they are far ahead in the classroom. By bringing these two groups together, the overprivileged (whites) can help the underprivileged (blacks).

Adult professionals that work in the educational arena are plagued by disadvantages. By far White educators are the norm when teaching at the college level. According to *underrepresented women in higher education:* "as of 2005 approximately 1% Of full time professors were Black, 1% were Asian, 0.6% were Hispanic and 0.1% were Native American"(Roberts, Agosto Pg.7).[15]

---

[14]Rothstein, Richard."why are our schools segregated."Educational Leadership.May2013,Vol.70 Issue 8,p50-55.6p.Aceademic search complete.

[15]Cobb-Roberts, Deirdre, and vonzell Agosto. "Underrepresented women in higher

This number means over 98% of full time college educators are White. The odds of African Americans becoming full time college professors are less than 2%. If this does not tell us something is wrong with America, then I do not know what does. This epidemic follows women on a gender level as well. Women find it much harder to clinch college level teaching positions, and the majority of college educators are men. Surveys have been taken to try and figure out the level of difficulty Black female professor's face in the teaching arena. They find it much harder to achieve promotions and tenure based off their actual work performance. They are mostly evaluated on the basis that they are female and Black. This kind of evaluation can isolate Black female professors and devalue the work they do. Why are Black females viewed as less valuable than their male White counter parts? Furthermore, why are the majority of college educators White?

There has been a drastic increase in the amount of African American students that are home schooled. This approach to education which was once perceived to be a fad, has now grown into a new form of education. More African Americans are being home schooled than ever before. The number of African

education: An overview." Negro education review 62/63.1-4 (2011):7-11. Academic search complete. Web. 28 may 2012

Americans being home schooled has increased from 10% in the late 1990's to 15% as of 2012. Why are African Americans increasingly keeping their children at home and away from the educational institution so many Americans put their faith in? For some, it is simply because they are dissatisfied with the educational curriculum developed by this country. For others they want their children to have the necessary family attention, but for the vast majority of African American parents that home school their children it is because of Racism. According to the article *African American Homeschooling as Racial Protectionism:* "15 African American home schooling families, mentioned that they are tired of the racist, sexist, propaganda that masquerades as the truth in history textbooks"(Mazama, Lundy 725).[16] These parents agreed that racial protection played a significant role in their decision to keep their children home schooled. "White educators often treat African American students different than white students, showing negative attitudes towards black children at times and African Americans are usually targeted for punishment in school more often than whites"(Mazama, Lundy 726).[17]

The lack of African history and the profusion of White

---

[16]Mazama, Ama, and Garvey Lundy. " African American Homeschooling As Racial Protectionism." Journal Of Black Studies 43.7 (2012):723-748.

[17]Mazama, Ama, and Garvey Lundy. " African American Homeschooling As Racial Protectionism." Journal Of Black Studies 43.7 (2012):723-748.

history in public school curriculums only further reassures the notion that this society sees Africa and all other cultures as inferior. This Racist curriculum leads Black children to believe their Race has not achieved much, which is a complete lie. This country would be barren without Black people. African Americans contributions have made America a stronger nation. Without Black people hundreds of inventions so many White Americans rely on today would not exist. The curriculum African Americans have relied on for so long has been designed to ensure Black students remain oblivious to who they are, and conditioned to believe they have nothing to offer the world.

According to *African American Home schooling as racial protectionism:* "white teachers often participate consciously or unconsciously in the marking of whiteness as inevitable, colorless and as the inevitable norm"(Mazama, Lundy727).[18] In other words, White educators usually bring negative stereotypes with them of African Americans into the classroom, treating Black students different than White students. We can examine school punishment and how it is completely different for Whites and Blacks. Black schools predominately have much more security, metal detectors, and armed guards ready to search African

---

[18]Mazama, Ama, and Garvey Lundy. " African American Homeschooling As Racial Protectionism." Journal Of Black Studies 43.7 (2012):723-748.

American students for weapons, drugs, and guns, which creates the perception that Blacks are dangerous and need constant supervision. White schools have more school shootings and massacres every year compared to Black schools. Every time there is a shooting in a White school there is an increase in security in Black schools. According to a report issued by *the Southern Poverty Law Center* "black male students are today over three times more likely than white students to be suspended from school and black females are four times more likely than white females to be suspended "(Mazama, Lundy729).[19] African Americans are treated as criminals in the school system. Armed guards and constant searches, prepares Black students for a life of being searched and monitored by law enforcement officers. Students are subjected to random searches, which is illegal and a violation of their fourth amendment right. Society trains young African American men and women about what their lives will be like when they are adults, by ensuring the educational institutions African Americans learn from mirror that of prison. Predominantly White schools have much less security, and the majority of them do not have scanners and cops waiting to greet them at the front door.

---

[19]Mazama, Ama, and Garvey Lundy. " African American Homeschooling As Racial Protectionism." Journal Of Black Studies 43.7 (2012):723-748.

On January 8th, 1991, Jeremy Wade Delle killed himself with a .357 magnum in front of his second period English class in Richardson, Texas. May 1st, 1992, Eric Houston killed 4 people and wounded 10 more in a massacre that left Olivehurst, California shocked. January 18th, 1993, Scott Pennington walked into his classroom shot his teacher and school custodian, then managed to hold his classmates hostage. November 15th, 1995, James Rouse killed a student and teacher, and seriously wounded another teacher with a .22 caliber rifle. October 1st, 1997, Luke Woodham only developed the mental capacity to murder his mother, ex-girlfriend, and another student while wounding seven other students at Pearl High School in Pearl, Mississippi. May 21, 1998 Kip Kinkel killed his parents, drove to his high school, shot and killed two more students and wounded another 25 students in Springfield, Oregon. April 20th, 1999, Eric Harris and Dylan Klebold killed 12 students one teacher and wounded another 21 students before turning the weapons on themselves and committing suicide; this occurred in Columbine, Colorado. On March 21, 2005, Jeffrey Weise killed his grandfather and his grandfather's companion, drove his grandfather police car to Red lake high school shot and killed 5 students, one teacher, a security guard, and wounded 7 other students before committing suicide. February 14th, 2008, Steven Kazmierczak shot multiple people in a classroom of Northern Illinois University. He killed 5 people and wounded another 21 students before turning the weapon on himself. February 27, 2012, Thomas Lane went to his high school and opened fire on a group of students sitting at a cafeteria table, killing 3 and wounding 3 other students. Adam Lanza killed his mother, drove to Sandy Hook Elementary School and opened fire on first grade students, killing 20 first graders, 4 teachers, the principal, and the school psychologist in Connecticut. Let's not forget Christopher Harper Mercer, who on October 1, 2015 performed a mass school shooting killing 9 students and injured 9 others. This left Roseburg Oregon devastated. Every school shooting that was just listed was undertaken by a White individual. Whites can do whatever they want without ever having to worry about their actions ascribing to their race. Racism provides the social support that allows White Americans to continuously undertake actions no other race would get away with doing.

Black students are highly overrepresented in special education classes and terribly underrepresented in advanced placement classes. Black students that do well on examinations are often accused of cheating. Based on the article *African Americans in schools: Tiptoeing around Racism:* they list five facets where educational Racism exist in one school that decided to create a program aimed at increasing the grades of African Americans in science and mathematics.

"1.) the district should retain students who have not mastered grade level curricula; then I can do my job effectively, 2.) Focusing on black students, I am ignoring the rest, so I reject the project, 3.) Other people need to be responsible first, then I'll do my part, such as the parents and previous teachers, 4.) The child had a deficit, and 5.) The system perpetuates low expectations" (Rozansky-Lloyd 598).[20] Each excuse adds to the educational discrimination so many African Americans have to deal with on a daily basis. Excuse one tries to place the blame on the system so that teachers do not have to take responsibility for not aggressively helping these struggling students. Excuse two does not make sense because for the most part African Americans are ignored in the classroom, so focusing on them will actually level out the playing field. Excuse three basically says that because everyone else is not helping, that gives teachers the right to also not help, which makes absolutely no sense. Excuse four tries to define African Americans as having a learning disability; that they naturally learn slower than other races, which obviously is not supported by any empirical data. And finally, excuse five which says the system basically preserves low expectations, assumes

[20]Rozansky-Lloyd, Carol. "African Americans In Schools: Tiptoeing Around Racism." Western Journal Of Black Studies 29.3(2005): 595-604. Academic Search Complete. Web.12 June 2013.

Black students aim low in academics and never strive for success in the classroom. These Racist perceptions, and ideologies of African Americans are the underlying reasons Black students struggle much more than White students in school.

The City University of New York was founded in 1847 and only had 143 students. The University allowed students to get a higher education for free. Low income Americans that could not afford college were finally able to get an education without having to spend thousands of dollars. Since then CUNY has evolved to over 270,000 students that are working on degrees ranging from Liberal Arts to Economics. Today CUNY is no longer free but cost substantially lower than other private institutions. CUNY became a way out for many African Americans seeking to become academically competitive and technically skilled in a tough labor market.

During the mid-1990's New York City elected Rudolph Giuliani for Mayor, and one of his primary goals were limiting African Americans access to College. He basically declared war on CUNY. Former Mayor Giuliani wanted to eliminate remedial courses throughout CUNY and declared that underprepared students did not belong in college. He also threatened to yank away all city funding from CUNY if the colleges refused to comply with his demands. College is a place for students to learn, if unprepared students do not belong in college (a place of learning), where exactly do they belong? And if these so called unprepared students cannot keep up in college level classes, then that is exactly what remedial courses are there for; to get them prepared for college level work. It is no surprise the majority of students in remedial classes are African Americans and Hispanics. By eliminating remedial courses Giuliani would be exiling thousands of African Americans and Hispanics, who were not yet able to compete in college level classes, but none the less wanted to succeed in college. According to the article *New York Mayor declares war on CUNY:* Dr. Antonio Perez, who is the President of The Borough of Manhattan Community College said "about half of all students need at least one remedial course".[21]

Giuliani continued his campaign and rampage of verbally humiliating the CUNY system to scare the colleges into eliminating all remedial courses. During Giuliani's reign "CUNY records showed that 55% of all freshmen entering into the community colleges were not recent high school graduates and more than 56 percent did not speak English as their first language."[22] It only makes sense to have these remedial courses

---

[21]Wright, Scott W.,"New York Mayor Declares War on CUNY."Community College week.02/09/98,Vol.10 issue 14, p2. 1/5p.Academic Search Premier.
[22]Wright, Scott W.,"New York Mayor Declares War on CUNY."Community College week.02/09/98,Vol.10 issue 14, p2. 1/5p.Academic Search Premier.

available to help these students perform at grade level. Giuliani's policies not only affected African Americans but anyone who was not raised on White traditionally norms. According to the article *This isn't working:* "At the Borough of Manhattan Community College more than half of the students come from households with income below $20,000 a year and most students are forced to work full or part-time jobs."[23] By eliminating remedial courses Giuliani would be excluding African Americans from the University. He wanted the numbers on paper to reflect progress, even if progress was not really being achieved. If it meant getting rid of Blacks and other low socioeconomic individuals that were pulling the numbers down, then so be it. If the former mayor really cared about progress he would not have attacked CUNY, but attacked the problem at the source; which is our repulsive educational system that failed to prepare these students for college in the first place. His administration should have advised him to change the organizational structure of our education system, instead he chose to attack an institution designed to create opportunities for those who have constantly been denied it.

Critical Race Theory is an academic term used to examine society, culture, race, law, and power. This theory analyzes Racism

[23]Wright, Scott W., "This isn't working." Black Issues in Higher Education. 02/19/98, Vol. 14 issue 26, p14. 2p. 3 Black and White Photographs. Academic Search Premier.

and recognizes that it is implanted in the roots of our society. It is used to analyze the structure of society and ensures that this structure is based on White Privilege and White Supremacy. **Critical Race Theory** suggest that Racism is a normal part of American life. There will never be a color blind society. Decisions concerning equality will always be race based, sometimes consciously or unconsciously. If there was a Color blind society that would mean African Americans and other targeted Racial Minorities would have an equitable chance of obtaining career goals. That would mean more African Americans would be able to go college, and enigmas that work to the detrimental effects of Blacks would no longer exists. America would never allow this to happen because Racism is the one tool used to give Whites an edge over Blacks. It is a tool used to create privilege and status. We are fully aware that status is one of the most important values ingrained into American society. According to UCLA: "The individual racist need not exist to note that institutional Racism is pervasive in the dominant culture."[24] This means that individual Racism is no longer important to maintain this status quo of White Privilege because institutions are making snap decisions based solely on participant's skin color. This suggest that all

---

[24]UCLA School of Public Affairs Critical race
Studies.http://spacrs.wordpress.com/what-is-critical-race-theory/

institutions like higher education institutions are Racist.

CRT rejects the idea of meritocracy. **Meritocracy** is a philosophy that believes individuals advance in society based on demonstrated achievements and intellectual superiority. CRT rejects this idea and believes that this idea is false. This philosophy was developed by people of wealth and power to condition individuals into believing that by working hard power, wealth and status can be achieved, while ignoring the application of Racism. Racism cannot be ignored, it is our culture; a system of values and norms we use that dictates the way we behave. By applying Racism into our life, meritocracy does not hold true. Regardless of how hard we work, the majority of African Americans will never achieve wealth, power, and status.

The number of African Americans enrolled in law schools are stagnate. To be considered for law school each applicant must obtain a four year college degree, score well on the Law School Admissions Test and maintain adequate grades throughout their undergraduate career. Statistics show African Americans are less likely to be admitted to law school programs. There are approximately 50 million African Americans in the United States of America and according to the article *the Misuse of Law School Admissions Test* "Only 9,681 Blacks were enrolled in law school programs across the country in 1994."(pg. 168)[25] The sad part is, this is the peak of Black student enrollment of any year in this country. In 2004 the number of African Americans enrolled in law schools across the country decreased to only 9, 488 students. The LSAT is used as the primary factor for law school admissions. By examining California law schools we see they actually raised the average score for admission by 2.8 points which led to a decline in the number of Blacks enrolled in law schools in California. New York law schools are worse; they raised the average LSAT score by over 3 points which lead to a 21.6% decline in African American enrollment. According to the Law School Admissions Council (LSAC) "the LSAT should be used as one of several criteria's for evaluation and should not be given undue weight solely because it is convenient."(pg.175)[26] Over the years the LSAT has become the strongest determinant of law school admissions. By giving undue weight to LSAT scores, law schools are actually denying qualified African Americans acceptance into their schools.

According to an article published in the Harvard Crimson

[25]Nussbaumer, John. "MISUSE OF THE LAW SCHOOL ADMISSIONS TEST, RACIAL DISCRIMINATION, AND THE DE FACTO QUOTA SYSTEM FOR RESTRICTING AFRICAN-AMERICAN ACCESS TO THE LEGAL PROFESSION."St. John's Law Review. Winter2006, Vol. 80 Issue 1, p167-181-F. 21p.Academic Search Premier

[26]Nussbaumer, John. "MISUSE OF THE LAW SCHOOL ADMISSIONS TEST, RACIAL DISCRIMINATION, AND THE DE FACTO QUOTA SYSTEM FOR RESTRICTING AFRICAN-AMERICAN ACCESS TO THE LEGAL PROFESSION."St. John's Law Review. Winter2006, Vol. 80 Issue 1, p167-181-F. 21p.Academic Search Premier

"There is some combination of cultural bias on the LSAT exam and atmosphere bias."(thecrimson.com)[27] The author Kidder, explains that stereotypes that work to damaging effects of African Americans can actually limit and depress their performance on these standardized exams. The LSAT is bias because Blacks and Whites essentially take different courses throughout their lifetime. Whites are given courses that prepares them for standardized exams while Blacks are not. By giving African Americans an examination they have never been fully prepared for and placing greater importance every year on that very same exam, limits the ability of African Americans to being accepted into Law schools.

---

[27]http://www.thecrimson.com/article/1998/10/2/report-shows-lsat-score-gap-pa/

Testimonies on Education

Sex: Male
Age: 24
Race: African American

"When I was a junior in college I was taking a micro-economics course that I disliked over all my other courses. At the time, I was the only African American in the class and I felt that my professor would constantly ignore me. He constantly asked if we had any questions and every time I raised my hand he looked over me and continued with the lesson. I'm sure I was not the only student that began noticing this. Whether I raised my hand for a question or to participate, either way I rarely got any response back from my professor. I practically had to teach myself microeconomics for that term. I ended up with a B- in the class, but I'm sure that if this teacher showed me the same respect as any other student in the class, I would have gotten a better grade."

Sex: Male
Age: 45
Race: African American

"I was scheduled to have an advisory appointment with my J.H.S. counselor as an 8th grader to discuss what H.S. I should apply to. I went to Ms. Seiden's office at the appointed time, sat down and she asked me what I wanted to be. I told her that I wanted to design buildings because I liked building things as a child. She sat for a moment and then said "You know plumbers make good money". I said "I know I have carpenters and plumbers in my family and they do live well, but I want to be an architect". She went on to explain how hard it was to become an architect. I had been in 7sp and 8sp which were top classes so I was use to hard work, so at first I did not understand her point. But even at that young age I left her office knowing she did not have my best interest at heart and it made me angry. I applied and got into Brooklyn Technical High School and graduated on time. I did not become an architect but I did gain a valuable experience regarding design and ended up designing a line of jewelry, note cards and logos.

Sex: Female
Age: 20
Race: African American

"When entering college I knew this would be an experience to remember. I was the only black student in the class and everyone would constantly looked to me for my opinion. Not only in class did I feel uncomfortable, but also on campus. I realized soon how I was being portrayed by other students that were not black. I felt that students stereotyped me into this category of "the typical black girl". I remember hanging out on campus with some classmates. A white student I met a few times walked over and said a normal hello to everyone and when he approached me, he did all this hip hop talk and movement just to say hi to me. Everyone else giggled and nudged me to laugh, he was laughing as well while trying to give me a hand shake. I responded with a normal hello. I couldn't believe it. Why was it he felt it was ok to talk normal to everyone else and speak street slang to me? He assumed that was how I behaved on a normal basis and would be acting white if I did not. I didn't address it at the time but later I thought about it a little more and realized it did bother me. He assumed that's how I greet people and it definitely was not."

Sex: Male
Age: 21
Race: African American

"I was headed to my college gym one day and had on sweat pants and a t-shirt. From my understanding this was normal gym attire. By chance I happened to run into a professor at my school who happened to be the chairman of the political science department. He was with another professor; a white woman that I never met before. It was weird that they were having a full conversation about me before I ran into them. When I arrived at both professors I tried shaking the hands of the white professor but she barely wanted to touch me. It wasn't until the chairman told her who I was that she actually wanted to look at me. The chairman said "it's so funny we were just talking about you" He went on and told her I was the student he was referring to 10 minutes ago, the full scholarship student that maintained a very high GPA. I could see her look at me in surprise to hear all the wonderful academic credentials I had. I merely gave her a smirk, shook the chairman's hand and kept walking. I remember thinking to myself why was she was so eager to write me off as scum when I didn't do anything to her. It was sad and also racist to judge me completely off my skin color and the way I dress rather than who I am as a person."

Sex: Male
Age: 25 years old
Race: African American

"I was taking a Statistics course at my college during my junior year. I found the course to be relatively easy. One day my professor was having a discussion about probability and he was examining the ins and outs of how to really analyze this particular topic. He was using examples from the real world to further emphasize his points. He pointed to a white student and described the probability her getting into a college based on how many schools she applied for. He pointed to another white male and discussed the probability of rolling a certain number had he been gambling with dice. My professor then pointed at me, and analyzed the probability of me being arrested. I was so shocked that he chose to use such a topic when comparing and analyzing probability for me. The other black students in the classroom looked on in dismay as he used the example of jail to describe probability for me. I kept wondering in my mind why he chose that topic for me and other normal non-criminal topics for the white students in the classroom. I wanted to speak to him after class about the comment but I didn't want to put my grade at risk, so I ignored it and focused the rest of the term on finishing strong in the class."

2.

Finding employment in America is challenging enough without the heavy scrutiny of Racism. Candidates are rarely hired based on their qualifications and Americans are led to believe hiring based on racial identity is a lie. A close examination of surveys presented on the perception of African Americans and Hispanics that deal with Racial Discrimination on a daily basis indicates that racial biases exists within the employment sector. According to the article *Sociology of Discrimination: Racial Discrimination in Employment, Housing, Credit and Consumer Markets* "A 2001 survey found that more than one third of Blacks and nearly 20% of Hispanics reported they personally been passed on because of race or ethnicity"(Pager, Shepherd 182).[28] That's 33% of Blacks being judged, not on their qualifications but by their skin color.

Discrimination can lead to African Americans performance in school, and labor market participation to decline. If African Americans believe they will not find a good job after they graduate, they will not work as hard in school, creating the perception that Black students are incompetent. If the only jobs

---

[28] Pager, Devah, and Hana Shephred. "The Sociology Of Discrimination: Racial Discrimination In Employment, Housing, Credit and Consumer Markets." Annual Review Of Sociology 34.1(2008): 181-209. Academic Search Complete.web.17 June 2013.

available to African Americans are low wage jobs then a large portion of African Americans will not participate in the labor force, which feeds into stereotypes of Blacks being lazy. Though this country has come a very long way in terms of jobs African Americans can compete for, there are still huge wage gaps between Whites and Blacks. "African Americans are twice as likely to be unemployed as Whites, and wages of both Blacks and Hispanics continue to lag behind those of Whites"(Pager, Shepherd 187).[29] Studies have shown that individuals with White names compared to African American names experience higher call back rates when submitting resumes for job positions. "White names triggered a call back rate that was 50% higher than that of equally qualified Black applicants"(Pager, Shepherd 187).[30] With disadvantages like these it has become the norm that most African Americans maintain low income, and low level authority positions.

In a case audit study by Bendick, he found that amongst White and Black test applicants, Whites were offered 15 cents per

[29] Pager, Devah, and Hana Shephred. "The Sociology Of Discrimination: Racial Discrimination In Employment, Housing, Credit and Consumer Markets." Annual Review Of Sociology 34.1(2008): 181-209. Academic Search Complete.web.17 June 2013.

[30] Pager, Devah, and Hana Shephred. "The Sociology Of Discrimination: Racial Discrimination In Employment, Housing, Credit and Consumer Markets." Annual Review Of Sociology 34.1(2008): 181-209. Academic Search Complete.web.17 June 2013.

hour higher than their equally qualified Black test partner (Pager, Shepherd 187).[31]

The longer candidates are unemployed, the less likely they are to develop new skills crucial to them staying competitive in the labor market. People who are unemployed face a wide range of issues. Unemployment can lead parents to develop alcoholism and commit suicides. If Blacks are twice as likely to be unemployed than Whites, this means Blacks are twice as likely to experience more drinking addictions and suicides to cope with being unemployed compared to Whites. This leads to more African American children growing up with alcoholic parents or without father's at all because their father either committed suicide or left since they could not cope with being unemployed. Racially discriminating against minorities in the labor market not only impacts the individual but it impacts everyone that individual has connections to.

There has been great research done in the area of analyzing involuntary job dismissal amongst African Americans and Whites. By using surveys and statistical data, researchers have produced interesting findings. According to *Race and Job Dismissal: African*

---

[31] Pager, Devah, and Hana Shephred. "The Sociology Of Discrimination: Racial Discrimination In Employment, Housing, Credit and Consumer Markets." Annual Review Of Sociology 34.1(2008): 181-209. Academic Search Complete.web.17 June 2013.

American/white Differences in Their sources During the Early Work Career "nearly twice the portion of African Americans (28%) as whites (15%) in the entire sample experienced involuntary job loss."(Wilson 1189).[32] The job dismissal rate remained the same when analyzing the working class and the middle class. The jobs African Americans manage to get are less unionized and have fewer benefits. These numbers assert that socioeconomic status plays a major determinant in the positions we hold in society. Basic demographic features determine what jobs an individual will get. Characteristics like race, income level, credit scores, and social status become the determining factors of being hired. Any management professor or hiring manager will assert that there is "supposed" to be a specific process used to identify a candidate for a position. There are 5 steps in the selection process of a candidate, "1.)Screening applications and resumes, 2.)Testing and reviewing work samples, 3.)Interviewing candidates, 4.)Checking references and background, and 5.)Making a selection."(Noe, Hollenbeck, Gerhart, Wright 192).[33] In theory, this process makes a great deal of sense because it examines the entire candidate and what skills the candidate can bring to the organization. When

---

[32]Wilson, George. "Race And Job Dismissal: African American/White Differences In Their Sources During The Early Work Career." American Behavioral Scientist48.9 (2005): 1182-1199. Academic Search Complete. Web. 17 June 2013

[33]Noe, Hollenbeck, Gerhart, wright. Fundamentals of Human resource Management. New York: McGraw Hill/Irwin, 2011.

Racism and Discrimination is intertwined with this process, African Americans do not make it pass step 2. Instead of choosing applicants based on their resumes, references, aptitude scores, cognitive ability, job performance skills, and drug results, applicants are scored by their skin color, and how ethnic their names sound. How can racial minorities achieve greatness in a society designed like this? It is wrong for companies to pursue actions that contribute toward the extensive degradation of African Americans.

Affirmative Action is a policy that was created to protect under-represented minority groups. The policy takes factors such as an individual's race, religion, and sex into account when representing them in employment and business. The policy was developed to promote opportunities for minorities. The Fire Department has been under attack by Racism since the 1980's. The International Association of Fire Fighters (I.A.F.F), which has over 177,000 members in its union, is one of the most Racist organizations in the employment sector. In the 1980's the I.A.F.F collected funds from their union members (both White and Black), then used those funds to finance lawsuits against minority programs. What's more appalling is that during the 1980's, there were over 13,000 Black fire fighters in the I.A.F.F and not one of them were on the executive board.[34] All board members for the fire department were White. Blacks held lower paying and lower level authority positions. Miami is the best example of how Racist the Fire Department is. According to *Fighting the Fires of Racism* [In 1964 the first African American was hired to be a fire fighter in Miami. And then it took another 6 years just to hire two more black fire fighters.... After the establishment of (I.A.B.F.F) the International Association of Black Fire Fighters and a thorough investigation, the federal district court concluded that Blacks were purposely excluded from employment and other advancement opportunities in the fire department. Rockwell 714][35]

Life for African Americans in the fire department was a living hell because they were subjected to the harsh harassment of other White fire fighters. The late 1980's was a defining period for African Americans. Naturally the I.A.F.F saw the I.A.B.F.F as a threat and as a result fired all African Americans within the department of Miami in 1988. This was after these African Americans paid thousands of dollars in dues. The actions of the fire department mirrors the American government. African Americans pay millions in taxes every year and receive very little political, economic and social support from the American

[34]Rockwell, Paul. "Fighting The Fires Of racism." Nation249.20(1989): 714-718. Academic Search Complete.Web. 17 June 2013
[35]Rockwell, Paul. "Fighting The Fires Of racism." Nation249.20(1989): 714-718. Academic Search Complete.Web. 17 June 2013

government. Like the fire department, the American Government taxes racial minorities and gives them nothing in return. The 1980's, Affirmative Action and the I.A.B.F.F paved the way for African American fire fighters in 2016 to maintain their current positions.

The ability to increase the output each worker produces increases revenue, profits, gross margin, and shareholders wealth. One substantial way to increase productivity is for firms to invest in their human capital. **Human Capital** are the skills, knowledge and capabilities of the human resources that helps to produce goods and services for a firm. Providing human resources with the right training, and promotional opportunities, will give them the push they need to be more productive in the workplace. Understanding how individuals feel through career opportunity distribution, firms can make better decisions to what workers need to make them more productive. Creating a stable work environment that includes unbiased opportunities for all employees will increase productivity within an organization. African Americans have a negative perception of opportunities in the workplace. When measuring leadership abilities, Whites are believed to have innate leadership abilities while Blacks are believed to have to develop these skills. With the perception that Whites are naturally better at leadership roles than African

Americans, resources and time invested in White employees are not the same as resources invested in African Americans.

Networking plays a significant role in achieving upward mobility. Because most African Americans are all but cut off from these networking opportunities, their chances of mobility within an organization are slim. "It's not what you know, it's who you know" and in a competitive labor market, without the ability to effectively network with top management how can African Americans move up within an organization? In 2008 women and minorities received fewer rewards than White males having similar performance appraisals. Without the ability to effectively network, minorities will find it harder to get promotions and raises in salary, which leads to lower income in the Black economy. Many African Americans are cheated out of a fair salary every year, based on an assumption that they are getting paid equal to their White counterparts working the same position. Of those Blacks that are happy with their pay, the majority of them do not know how much their White counter parts are being paid for the same position. Fifty percent of Whites are paid more than their Black correspondents that are working the same position, and most African American employees would never know they are getting paid less because discussing salary is prohibited in most organizations.

Whenever the nation experiences any economic downturn, racial minorities suffer more than anyone else. In times of recessions, the African American unemployment rate usually sky rockets. It can reach heights of up to 51% unemployment for Blacks and other racial minorities. It is the job of political leaders not to sit on the sidelines and hope the market corrects itself, but for these leaders to correct the market and create opportunities everyone can benefit from. If 51% of Blacks are unemployed for extended periods of time, you can picture the impairment it does to the Black community.

People accept or stay at a position because of inducements. Inducements such as power and personal advancements, coined with money and security are great reasons as to why people take on certain roles. There are two inducements that play leading roles in African Americans decision in accepting a job. The first is whether the White employer has been conditioned to believe that Blacks are beneath them and without Affirmative Action, Blacks would not have the jobs they have now, regardless of their degrees. The second is people like to be around others that resemble themselves, and because African Americans are culturally different than Whites, it is difficult for Blacks to fit in.

The amount of nominal wages that have been lost due to unequal workplace opportunities are in the billions. African

Americans are usually required to meet more intricate criteria's than Whites when applying for a position; such as more degrees, more experience, and taking part in longer interviews. To get an idea of how bad it is, according to Tim Wise, a distinguished sociologist "the average white family has 12 times the accumulated net worth of the average African American family and 8 times the net worth of an average Latino family"[36]. Because of this accumulation, White families with less than $15,000 a year in net income are better off than well-educated African Americans that make over $60,000 a year in net income. Whites have more material assets than Blacks which is really what matters in the long run, not money.

Black women experience discrimination, both because of their gender and their skin color. They are viewed as incompetent and unable to carry out basic tasks. According to the article *Black Women Talk About Workplace Stress and How They Cope* "there are five basic triggers that stress black women in the workplace; being hired or promoted, developing relationships with coworkers, dealing with Racism and Discrimination, being isolated or excluded, and changing to overcome barriers to employment"(pg. 213)[37] Black women have to change who they are completely if

---

[36]Pathology of the white privileged. Tim Wise. Youtube.2007

[37]Khosrovani, Masoomeh, and James W. Ward. "African Americans perception Of Access To Workplace Opportunities: A survey Of employees in Houston Texas."

they want to be promoted in today's world. The vast majority of Black women are conditioned to take on European values as their own and wholly believe these so called values are theirs, when in fact it is because of Racism Black women think the way they do.

To advance within an organization, African American women are forced to assimilate to achieve workplace mobility. Black parents begin early stages of assimilation, by relaxing their daughter's hair. Using chemical relaxers to straighten ones hair can cause extraordinary damage to the scalp. The chemicals break down the protein and nutrients in a woman's hair leaving burned edges, and baldness. They have been conditioned to believe that straight hair is beautiful and that workplace mobility can only be achieved through this dangerous process. African American women with natural hair find it much harder to land positions than women with relaxed hair.

Women are the backbone of our civilization. They give birth to the future population that matures to manage and upkeep our economy. On average women are still paid less than their male counterparts performing the same job. Households are becoming increasingly single parented. Single moms are becoming the norm when raising children. Black women experience difficulty in

Journal Of Cultural Diversity 18.4(2011):134-141.Academic Search Complete.Web13 Jan. 2014.

securing powerful, authority held positions compared to White women with the same amount of education and qualifications. Black women typically land jobs that are female oriented which pays lower than other professions.

One of the key issues frequently discussed by Barack Obama during his Presidential campaign was unemployment. It is the President's job to broadcast to the American people the unemployment rate that currently exists. According to an article by CNSnews; data used by Obama suggested the unemployment rate fell to about 7.8% in August 2013.[38] The Bureau of Labor Statistics (BLS) calculates the unemployment rate by using three criteria's: those who are out of work, those who are capable of working and those who are actively seeking employment. This means if candidates cease their pursuit for employment because they are discouraged from not finding a job, they will not be included in the data for unemployment. The unemployment figures reported are generally incorrect. The real unemployment rate is usually higher when you take into account discouraged workers. Presidents use lower unemployment data to obscure the view of the American people to believe our economy is doing better than it actually is. If politicians really cared they would act in

---

[38]http://cnsnews.com/news/article/michael-w-chapman/unemployment-rate-down-05-56-months-obama-became-president

a way that would help Americans.

According to an article written by *dailycaller.com*, the Obama family spent nearly $1.4 billion on Presidential perks since they have been in office. Perks such as housing, staffing, flying, and entertainment. How can one family spend that much money on perks and base their campaign on CHANGE? It is evident why our economy is constantly witnessing fluctuating unemployment rates, our commander in chief uses tax payer's money on himself and his family. It makes one wonder, how many other politicians within this corrupt government are ciphering off billions for themselves? With leaders like this at the helms of our political system, poverty and real unemployment will never decline. Of course the fictional data accessible to the American public will constantly change, but real variables that indicate the true state of this country will not. The disappointing piece is that compared to other nations America steals the most money for Presidential perks. In comparison to Great Britain only $57.8 million were spent on the "Royal Family", which is still outrageously insensitive, considering the average individual makes about $2 million dollars in their lifetime. Obama has spent enough money for 700 lifetimes his short time in office. If this money was spent efficiently there would not be such high unemployment rates, so many homeless people living on the streets, minorities on government assistance programs, and there would not be senior citizens working when they should be retired.

During Barack Obama's second Presidential campaign he debated Mitt Romney at Hofstra University. During the debate Obama was asked by a young student about his plans for creating jobs for Americans. People attend college to find great jobs after they graduate, but if there are no jobs most people would not bother with higher education because there would be no incentive. According to an article written by *politifact.com* President Obama said that he created nearly five million jobs since he has been in office as President of the United States of America.[39] The real question should be, who are these jobs going to? In a society without discrimination five million jobs would be remarkable because they would be properly dispersed throughout the economy to individuals who possess the accurate skills and Human capital needed to perform the job efficiently. Individuals would be hired based on their qualifications above anything else. But in this society, Racism, Racial Discrimination and White Privilege plays the leading role in who gets what. Creating five million jobs is remarkable, but if African Americans and other minorities have lower chances statistically of being hired for any of

---

[39]http://www.politifact.com/truth-o-meter/statements/2012/oct/17/barack-obama/barack-obama-says-his-administration-has-created-5/

these positions, then these opportunities will only benefit Whites. It does not matter how many jobs Obama creates, the majority of these opportunities will always go to White Americans because the probability of Black candidates obtaining a job when competing against White candidates are very slim. Everything Obama has done in his political career means very little because he is only attacking the symptoms that are impacting Americans. He needs to attack the causes of those symptoms, and the main cause is Racism.

Testimonies on Employment

Sex: Female
Age: 35 years old
Race: Black/Afro-Caribbean

"There are few experiences that stand out in both my academic and professional life where I have experienced discrimination. I think that one of the issues that can be akin is having my education and seniority in the workplace challenged because I am a minority. Let me explain….I have been teaching for the past 7 years. One day while I was at work, the former academic vice president was introducing a new professor in the Arts and Sciences department to the teachers in the staff room. She introduced me casually and coldly without speaking about my tenure at the job but when she came to my white counterpart in the same department she immediately glorified her as the most senior teacher with the best credentials (which she elaborated) and some of the activities that she had accomplished. There was a sense that she made her seem better and more accomplished than me. It was hurtful because it leaves you to question your value to the organization that you serve."

Sex: Female
Age: 28 years old
Race: Black

"Racism has affected me in employment because I used to work at Starbucks for over 3 years and was never promoted. I never called out, rarely late, and knew everything about the company; including beverages quality. I was the only African American in the store, and people that started working in the store after me would get promotions constantly. My general manager would always find something wrong when evaluating me to move up within the organization or to get a pay raise. At first I didn't think much of it until I came to work one day and saw a white girl I trained being trained as a shift supervisor three months after being hired, I then knew that Starbucks was not the place I wanted to be at because of the way they were treating me."

Sex: male
Age: 25 years
Race: Black/African Descent

"Racism has affected me a number of times, when I went to apply to a number of jobs. The reason is because I'm Black/African American with an Arabic name. It was times I'm sure I didn't get hired because of the way I look and my hair style as well. Not only are business owners racist but they are also sexist. I really dislike the fact that individuals have to pretend to be someone else just to get ahead in the employment world."

Sex: Male
Age: 23
Race: Black

"I remember when I was working at a brokerage firm. I was being trained to become a stock broker. This type of position requires both technical skills and decision making abilities. I was more of an intern than an actually employee. The first day the chief investment banker was asking everyone to go around and basically highlight themselves and explain why they think they can survive in a hostile environment like the stock market. They were only going to choose two interns at the end of the quarter to keep and train to get there series six license to trade stocks professionally. I was the only African American intern at the firm. So my boss went first and went on about how he was on an academic scholarship as an undergrad. All the other interns went and spoke highly of themselves and their skills. When it was my turn I also spoke about the fact that I was also on a full scholarship as well, but before I could finish my boss interrupted me and asked me a question I would never forget. He said "what Sport"? I had a really confused look on my face at first, but then it sunk in. He was asking me what sport I played to win a full scholarship. Not realizing that I actually won a full scholarship from my academic credentials and not from my physical jumping abilities, because there is no way that an African American can be on a full scholarship unless it was related to sports. I corrected him and told him that I didn't play any sports rather I won a business scholarship from my grades. He definitely had a puzzled facial expression and I knew then that I was working for a stereotypical, racist white man."

Sex: Male
Age: 24
Race: African American

"I never imagined that I would be asked to discuss such an occurrence, and the reason being that it's assumed that we now live in a fair more equal world. Or it is just possible that race is no longer an issue, it's all about class! My experiences beg to differ, and I'm sure I can find some people of my hue to agree. I have heard people refer to "HR" when the topic of race was ever mentioned. Just go to HR and tell them that something is going on, and they'll take care of it. As if that is supposed to quell the issue at hand. I can recall an instance of racism at a job that I have worked, where I worked as a door to door marketer. At this job my responsibility was to knock on every door on the block I was assigned until deceptively and effectively set three or more window/roof/siding appointments. These people lived in homes that were extravagant at times, and in other instances they lived in rundown shabby shacks. The condition of home never mattered when the right homeowners would open up, because their eyes said it all. Skeptical of what my intentions were in there affluent or at times all white neighborhoods, I would have people open up the doors look me up and down, and instantly slam the door in my face. This of course doesn't constitute as a racist act, because most solicitors, black or white hear doors slam on a regular basis. What made me feel as if these people were racist was the fact that if I had a white "handler" alongside me, it was deemed safe to be around the six foot 250 pounds giant. Standing outside of a door in a prominent neighborhoods, as the sun sets with my skin made selling these things nearly impossible. I managed to stay afloat for a bit, but decided that my fate was meek at best if I stuck around. Whether it's conscious or subconscious is not for me to say, the tension is there, and it was reality for me on the job every day."

Sex: Male
Age: 26
Race: African American

"I applied for a job at Northwestern Mutual, which is a financial company that deals with life insurance as well. My interviewer was a white lady that seemed very cheerful. She interviewed me for the position of a sales insurance agent at the company. I felt the interview went really strange. She asked me numerous questions about my career goals; both long term and short term and I remember she kept twisting my words; making it seem as if I was using slang throughout the interview. Every word that I used she kept saying thing like; did you say dope, or I'm sorry did you say iight. I remember thinking to myself that I'm speaking pretty clear, why is she making it seem as if I'm using words that a person from the streets would be using. I mean this was an interview, who in their right mind would come to a company this large and use language like that? Every time I corrected her she jotted things down on her note pad with a smirk on her face. She then told me after the interview was over that she would call me. Obviously I didn't get the job and I definitely felt that she had some type of prejudice attitude towards me because I was a young black man."

3.

Police Officers are citizens sworn in and empowered by the people to protect and enforce the laws laid out by the constitution of the United States. Their job is protect and serve the people of the nation to best of their ability. Police are supposed to be a symbol of hope, the ones citizens turn to when they are in fear and need help. The reality is, Police Officers are nothing more than a legalized gang, dispersed throughout the country to harass, kill, murder, and beat innocent minorities. Their only objective is to take advantage of those who cannot defend themselves. Cops have legal authority to lie to every citizen if it means setting them up for an arrest. For all those who still put their faith in law enforcement, it's time for you stop.

Kang Wong was beaten and left bloody by Police Officers in Jan. 2014 because of jay walking. Kang Wong is 84 years old, had no weapon on him and barely speaks English. The Police Officers that performed the beating are trying to convince America their lives were in such danger that almost a dozen of them had to beat Mr. Wong until he was left bloody. They then arrested Wong and charged him with assault. How could an unarmed 84 year old man possibly assault a young trained Police Officer who is armed with a gun? Ramarley Graham was shot and killed by Police in his own bathroom. Cops stalked him, kicked in his front door, entered his home without a warrant, went upstairs to his bathroom, pushed open the door and shot him point blank in the chest killing him instantly. They did all of this while his six year old brother watched in fear as his older brother was murdered before his eyes. The murdering officer said he was told Graham was armed and had drugs on him. No gun was found after the shooting. Trayvon Martin was murdered by George Zimmerman on Feb. 26, 2012. Zimmerman followed and stalked Martin for blocks, then engaged the young man after law enforcement told him not to. Zimmerman shot and killed Martin after a fight arose between the two. Zimmerman argued he followed Martin because he looked suspicious. Trayvon was wearing a hood and was carrying a candy in his hand at the time of the altercation. After the case went to trial, Martin's family failed to indict Zimmerman. Anyone with two eyes could see Martin was racially profiled when approached by Zimmerman. George argued the Stand Your Ground Law as to why he had to kill Young Trayvon Martin. This law authorizes a person to protect and defend one's own life and limb against threat or perceived threat. This law states that an individual has no duty to retreat from any place he/she has a lawful right to be and may use any level of force, including lethal, if he/she reasonably believes he/she faces an imminent and immediate threat. In Florida a

Black woman fired warning shots at her husband because she was scared of him, she did not kill him, nor did she injure him in any way. She argued the same Stand Your Ground Law Zimmerman argued and today she is facing 20 years in prison. Zimmerman on the other hand was set free for murder. Former tennis star James Blake was standing outside a New York hotel when an undercover NYPD cop grabbed and threw him to the ground before handcuffing and leading him away. The officer never identified himself, gave Mr. Blake the opportunity to give his name, nor read him his rights as every person who walks the streets are entitled to. What happened to James Blake is not uncommon in America. The vast majority of Police officer's conduct themselves in this very same way, it just so happen Officer James Frascatore got caught. On July 13th 2015, Sandra Bland was found dead in her cell at Waller County Jail in Texas. She was assaulted and arrested on July 10th for a traffic stop gone wrong. The White officer ordered Bland out of her car at gun point when she refused to put out her cigarette and assaulted her in a violent struggle. She was on her way to a job interview before she died in Police custody. On April 12th 2015, Freddy Gary was stopped by Police officers and beaten so badly he could not walk to the Police van. The officers can be seen on video dragging Mr. Gray instead of calling for medical services for the injured victim.

He was then arrested and thrown into the back of the Police wagon without being properly strapped in. The Officers proceeded to take Mr. Gray to Central bookings while being seriously injured from riding in the wagon without proper safety precautions. Gray died a week later from a broken vertebrae. The Officers involved face charges ranging from assault to second degree "depraved heart" murder. All the officers involved should be charged with first degree murder.

According to Tim Wise and the Department of Justice in a study released in 2004 "Black and Latino males are 3 times more likely to have their cars stopped and illegally searched by Police Officers for drugs, even though White males are 4.5 times more likely to actually have drugs on them on the occasion that they are stopped."[40] This suggests that Police Officers are racially profiling minorities instead of targeting criminals based on their actions. They are pulling over individuals because of their skin color instead of the suspicion of crime. In the eyes of the Police, African Americans driving luxury cars is reason enough for a traffic stop. Whites driving luxury cars is perceived as hard work transformed into success. This perception and way of thinking outs Police as Racist. These are people sworn in to protect and serve the general public but the true purpose of law enforcement is to instill and

---

[40] Pathology of the white privileged. Tim Wise. Youtube.2007

maintain fear in the minds of minorities. While Blacks are being pinned against the hood of their cars, hand cuffed to sit on curves and detained illegally for hours, White Americans are driving by without a care in the world because of the advantages provided to them by Racism.

Former Mayor Michael Bloomberg supports the "Stop and Frisk" law which is a complete violation of our Fourth Amendment right. He suggested that Police Officers are not racially profiling African Americans but are searching individuals that fit the profile of criminals. He argues a law that gives Police Officers the right to unjustly search another person is both efficient and unbiased to the public community. I wonder how the former Mayor would feel if Police stopped him every other day and searched him; if every time he saw a cop they pushed him against a car, spread his legs, told him to shut his mouth and searched him like a criminal. To support something as inhumane as this says a lot about Michael Bloomberg. Bloomberg stated that gun related crimes are mainly done by minorities and suspects of these crimes are usually identified as a minority. In fact he believes Whites are searched too often and minorities are not searched enough. If "Stop and Frisk" was the cause of low crime rates in New York City that means both crime and "Stop and Frisk" are related. Studies have shown that they are not. In fact when "Stop and Frisk" was reduced by 20% the crime rate did not rise at all, if they were related by decreasing searches the crime rate should have skyrocketed. Randomly searching innocent people does not lower crime it merely deteriorates the relationship between the public and law enforcement.

Day after day hundreds of minorities from New York City gather outside of the court houses for minor offensives. For years the NYPD, former Mayor Bloomberg and former Police Commissioner Ray Kelly has denied mandating ticket quotas to city cops for arrests and citations. But recently cops are coming forward to testify about the illegal activities occurring within the NYPD. According to ABC news reporter Jim Hoffer there are secret recordings of Police supervisors putting pressure on cops to meet quotas.[41] One New York City cop explains how he is directed to only stop Black and Hispanic teenagers and adults and perform routine illegal searches. The U.S constitution is supposed to provide protection for all Americans against unreasonable searches but it seems as if minorities are not considered Americans because their rights are constantly violated. The NYPD's criminal code states that an officer may stop a person when he reasonably suspects the individual has or is about to commit a crime. Eight year NYPD veteran Adrien Schoolcraft

---

[41] http://www.youtube.com/watch?v=rfJHx0Gj6ys

came forward and spoke about the illegal quotas NYPD officers are forced to meet at the 81st precinct. It became so bad, officers were starting to refer to their arrests as bodies. A common question used at this precinct was "how many bodies do you have in the cell?"[42] Schoolcraft secretly recorded supervisors pressuring him to hand out false tickets to innocent minorities walking the street. One supervisor said "you know what….. I stopped an asshole once; I gave him a $250 dollar ticket, what's the big deal?"[43] Bogus citations are flooding the New York City courts. According to Jim Hoffer court data suggest that in 2008 the courts handled 382,002 misdemeanor summonses and out of those 193,000 were tossed out by the courts.[44] That is nearly 51% of all summons deemed bogus and unwarranted by New York City Judges. Hoffer has received numerous emails from New York City cops stating that "command puts out a list every month, labeling officers without an arrest as a zero." This means these officers will be at risk of losing their jobs.

When Ray Kelly was deposed by community board officials about his Racist crime fighting tactics, he was lost at words. The data gathered from the NYPD "Stop and Frisk" program suggest that when NYPD officers frisk Whites they are getting more guns

---

[42] http://www.youtube.com/watch?v=rfJHIx0Gj6ys

[43] http://www.youtube.com/watch?v=rfJHIx0Gj6ys

[44] http://www.youtube.com/watch?v=rfJHIx0Gj6ys

off the streets than when they frisk Blacks percentage wise. Which begs the question; why are Blacks the target of "Stop and Frisk" when Whites are carrying more guns?

Federal Court Judge Shila Shyland slammed the city and the NYPD because of their Racist attitude towards minorities. She stated that "the NYPD has a Cavalier attitude towards the prospect of widespread practice of suspicionless stops and it displays a deeply troubling apathy to New Yorkers most fundamental constitutional rights."[45]

Sergeant Robert Berely of the Rockaway 100th precinct provided ABC News with extensive evidence to support his claim that the NYPD is cooking the data to make ethnic areas of New York City appear dangerous and White areas appear safer. Officers have come forward and testified that when people file reports to the NYPD, the next day when they come back to check on those reports; the complaint number is nowhere to be found. The NYPD also manipulate charges to make the city seem safer. When officers witness a felony crime and documents the report, that report is handed to the NYPD quality assurance department. This department then changes those charges to lesser crimes to make former Mayor Bloomberg and the Police Commissioner policies seem effective. Felonies and crimes

---

[45] http://www.youtube.com/watch?v=rfJHx0Gj6ys

committed in White areas are not recorded into Police database systems. The NYPD does not want to create the perception that White areas are dangerous. They manipulate the statistics by recording felony crimes in only predominantly Black neighborhoods. Because of this, one can suggest that White areas may actually have higher crime rates than Black areas, but because the NYPD refuses to record the incidents, it obscures the view of analyst readers.

In Los Angeles the LAPD has been skewing crime data for the past eight years. According to an article written by the Los Angeles Times "the LA Police Department misclassified 14,000 serious assaults as minor offenses from 2005 to 2012. Violent crime in the city was 7% higher than the LAPD reported and the number of serious assaults were 16% higher, the analysis found."[46] One of the cases misclassified was an incident involving a White woman name April L. Taylor. She was arrested and charged with assaulting her boyfriend with a deadly weapon back in 2009. For some reason her crime was reported in police database as a "simple assault". Even more disturbing, Bill Bratton; New York City's current Police Commissioner was LAPD's Police chief from 2002 to 2009. He led Los Angeles in falsifying information and Police dishonesty and is now running another major city.

---

[46] http://www.latimes.com/local/cityhall/la-me-crime-stats-20151015-story.html

Across the country we are witnessing extensive data manipulation by law enforcement institutions. This corrupt data is then used as the foundation for regulations restricting our basic constitutional rights.

Bloomberg ran an intense campaign against guns. The right to bear arms is in our constitution and a fundamental right of every American. He has made it difficult and near impossible for citizens of New York City to obtain legal fire arms to protect themselves. Basically Bloomberg only wants himself, the commissioner, and the NYPD to have access to guns, so they can harm and take advantage of New York City citizens without a fight.

Ninth precinct cop Nicolas Meana sold guns to the public for money and drugs. He sold stolen guns from the locker room of fellow Police Officers. Because these guns were being sold to drug dealers, the crimes committed in New York City increased. The very guns that officers are fighting to get off the streets are being placed there by cops. Bloomberg was caught selling 28,000 pounds of Police shells not to a recycle scrap metal company but to an ammunition company called Georgia arms.[47] Now why would a man who is so firmly against guns, bullets and the obtainment of such products by the general public, sell these

---

[47] http://www.youtube.com/watch?v=rfJHx0Gj6ys

products to a store where any individual can have access? He was basically supplying the public with bullets.

"Stop and Frisk" during the Bloomberg administration increased drastically each year. The number of shootings in NYC during the same time period also increased. If "Stop and Frisk" was an effective crime fighting tool, why is it that shootings across the city were higher than ever?

In 2010 The National Police Misconduct Statistics and Reporting Project, recorded over 6,613 Officers that were involved in abusing their duty of upholding the law.[48] The top three categories Officers tend to abuse their authority in are excessive force, sexual misconduct, and fraud/theft. Baton strikes, choking victims, taser related cases, and firearm cases are some examples of excessive force by officers. Darrin Manning; the 16 year old African American boy who is a straight A student was sexually assaulted by a female officer. She took it upon herself to squeeze Darren's buttocks and grab his testicles so hard; she popped it right off, leaving Darren in a wheelchair and possibly unable to ever bear children. Darren was charged with Aggravated Assault and resisting arrest. The data in the figure examines the different categories in which misconduct by law

---

[48]http://www.policemisconduct.net/2010-npmsrp-police-misconduct-statistical-report/

enforcement officers tends to take place, with excessive force accounting for almost 24% of all complaints filed.

Misconduct by Type

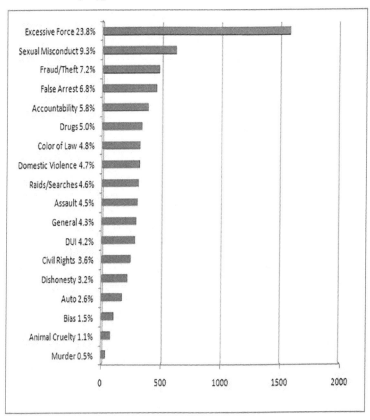

49

49http://www.policemisconduct.net/2010-npmsrp-police-misconduct-statistical-report/

In a public opinion survey, 89% of Blacks view the criminal justice system as biased against Blacks.[50] Tim Wise a distinguished sociologist and speaker on Racial Discrimination describes that Whites are in a constant denial about the impact their actions have on society and to minorities. According to Wise and a survey taken by White Americans, 16% of White Americans believed there is a fair chance Elvis is still alive. This number is ridiculous because when White Americans were asked if they felt Racism was still a significant issue in this country only 8% said yes.[51] This means Whites are twice as likely to believe Elvis is still alive then to believe Racism is still a significant issue in this country. As African Americans voice their complaints to politicians and corrupted Police officers, these complaints will never be taken seriously because White denial has become a way of life for White Americans.

Critical Race Theory Asserts that Racism is a part of our daily lives and analyzes how Racism is a natural part of our society. How can individuals who are targeted, beaten, murdered, and unjustly charged by law enforcement ever respect law enforcement? The relationship between minorities and Police

---

[50]Chaney,Cassandra , and Ray Robertson."Racism and Police Brutality In America."Journal of American Studies 17.4(2013):480-505.Academic search complete.Web.30 Mar.2014.

[51]Pathology of the white privileged. Tim Wise. Youtube.2007

Officers are deteriorating year after year. It is impossible for African Americans to ever have respect for law enforcement when they are the targets of misconduct from Police Officers.

Police Officers evolved from slave patrols to the modern day concept we see today. Slave patrols purpose was to protect property, but one very unique type of property. They were created to Police Black slaves in the southern states in the 1700s. They were ordered to hunt down and catch any runaway slaves that tried to escape their masters. These patrols were comprised of three to six White men determined to control and harm Blacks that did not follow or obey their rules. As the population of Black slaves increased the demand for slave patrols increased as well, creating more officers determined to control African slaves. Since slave patrols were only comprised of White men, it created massive issues for both Black slaves and free Black men. Free Black men were subjected to harassment, beatings, whipping, and arrest even when they did not break the law. The Patrol's mission were to detain and question all Blacks they encountered. Just as today, slave patrols would break up any large gatherings of Black men and commit illegal searches of these men. White slave owners constantly feared slaves would revolt, gather together and overthrow them; the pressure patrollers received from slave owners to keep Black slaves in check were extensive. Some Blacks fought back because of the constant Racist acts of these White slave patrol officers. The fugitive slave laws helped to create the formation of slave patrols. As in the 1700s, the targets of Police officers misconduct are African Americans. Cops harass, search and beat innocent minorities every day without any remorse, just as slave patrols did in the 1700s. Police officers today mirror law enforcement enacted during slavery.

Figuring out when the beginning of modern policing in the United States started is very difficult. We can use the mid-1800s as a marking point in which full-time paid officers were first created. *"The process of capitalist industrialization led to increasing economic inequality and exploitation and class stratification. Rioting became an essential political strategy of an underclass (a surplus population) and a working class suffering this increasing economic deprivation. The modern system of policing evolved to control this riotous situation."* (Eitzen, Timmer 1985)

Using a professional force to protect the people was mirrored from London's Metropolitan Police Department. After America saw what London developed, they did the same. Some of the responsibilities the U.S. took from the London police force are listed below:

1. The police exist to prevent crime and disorder.

2. Police must maintain public respect and approval in order to perform their duties.

3. Willing cooperation of the public to voluntarily observe laws must be secured.

4. Police use of force depends on the degree of cooperation of the public.

5. The police must be friendly to all members of society while enforcing the law in a non-biased manner.

6. Use of physical force should be used to the extent necessary to secure the compliance of the law.

7. Police are the public and public are the police.

8. Police should protect and uphold the law not the state.

9. Efficiency is measured by the absence of crime and disorder.

These nine points are to illustrate the vision of what Police officers are supposed to be like, but society has strayed very far from this original vision. Politicians use Police officers and other high ranked officials as they see fit, which ultimately creates corruption and favoritism within policing agencies.

Citizens should have an important role in the judgment of how Police offers are conducting themselves. For most of

America's history Police have conducted themselves without regarding the general public's view of their actions. Law enforcement officers have carried out actions for years, not concerned with what effects those actions will have on citizens. This is the main reason why the relationship between Police and citizens (mainly minorities) have reached a critical point.

Age is one of the biggest indicators used to determine citizen attitudes towards cops. Younger individuals seem to view Police officers as corrupt, evil, and predatory. Older citizens are usually the opposite; they view Police officers as impartial and tolerable. Research shows that individuals in lower social classes tend to view law enforcement as corrupt, Racist, and immoral. Those with less education and earn significantly lower salaries than most Americans view cops as being ruthless, compared to higher class individuals who earn more money annually tend to view Police officers as decent, respectable individuals.

The strongest determinant of public attitude towards law enforcement is Race and Ethnicity. African Americans and Latinos tend to view the actions of cops as shallow, and immoral, compared to Whites who normally perceive officer's actions as reasonable and justified. Contact with Police officers determines how individuals perceive officers and since African Americans are usually targeted by cops, their first encounter with officers usually begin with being assaulted, questioned, frisked, and often ignored. African Americans will then develop a negative mind set towards law enforcement because of officer's cavalier attitudes towards them. Whites on the other hand, are not targets of law enforcement, so their first encounters with cops usually begin and ends with handshakes and laughs. We can infer that law enforcement officers are not just targeting African Americans, but targeting a specific type of African American. Because anyone who is not young, anyone who is not African American, anyone who is not poor, and anyone who does not receive bad education typically are not subjected to the harsh reality of law enforcement discrimination.

<u>Testimonies on Police Discrimination</u>

Sex: Male
Age: 24
Race: African American

"The street that I live on was having a block party and everyone was having a good time. The community that I live in is predominantly filled with other blacks. At around 8pm white police officers walked onto my block and started telling everyone to go into their homes. The cops were shouting and pushing the people because they were hanging out on the sidewalk. The NYPD had no legal authority to tell the people to move and they arrested 5 African American men for refusing to go into their homes. I was one of them. I was charged with resisting arrest and obstruction of justice, whatever that is. I went from listening to music on my porch to sitting in a jail cell on trumped up charges from White cops. While in the jail cell, as I looked around what I noticed was 99% of everyone at central booking was an African American. I'm pretty sure the majority of people here were arrested for absolutely nothing. It also made me wonder, that of all the people in Brooklyn committing crimes, only black men were out there committing crimes..... REALLY!!"

Sex: Male
Age: 23
Race: African American

"I was walking down the street and was stopped by a white police officer. The cop asked me to show him ID and I told him no, that Brown Vs. Texas clearly states it is illegal for any public peace officer to ask for a citizen ID without some form of justification or suspecting me of committing a crime. He said if I didn't show him ID he was going to arrest me. I told him he had no legal authority to arrest me because I didn't do anything wrong, I was just stating the law. He attacked me and when I defending myself, I was handcuffed in a squad car. I was charged with resisting arrest, and causing a scene. The white cop called me a Nigga three times and said "that's what dumb Niggas get for acting up". Those who are sworn to protect and serve were speaking to a citizen like this. It's even on the side of their car; Respect, Professionalism, and courtesy. I felt like I was seconds away from being shot and ending up on the news as another black man killed by cops in Brooklyn. I figured going to jail is better than being killed by a white cop who was trying to measure his level of masculinity through abusing his powers as a police officer"

Sex: Male
Age: 24
Race: Black

"I was walking home late one night with my friend. We just came from our classmate's home. She was having a get together at her house. The house of the friend I just came from happen to be a white woman. The area we were walking in was predominately a white area in Brooklyn. I saw a police squad car zoom pass my friend and I, next thing I knew the cops made a complete illegal U-turn just to catch up to me and my friend. They drove half way on the side walk just to get to us then two white cops jumped out of the vehicle and told us to put our hands on the hood of the car. I asked what the problem was and what was it that we did? The cops pushed me against the car searched our pockets in front of everyone as if we were criminals. They kept shouting to keep our faces down on the car because I kept looking around as he was searching me. Then after they were done they said they got a call that someone got robbed. So because someone got robbed that must mean two black men walking down the street had to have done it? How pathetic is that? Even white bystanders were looking in awe as my friend and I were racially profiled because we were walking in a predominately white neighborhood. The cops said they were only doing their job. So I'm guessing that their job is to illegally harass, detain and search African Americans. I do not trust any cop Period."

Sex: Male
Age: 28
Race: African American

"Truthfully whenever I see the cops I always walk the opposite direction. I don't trust them nor do I need the stress that they provide in my life. The police are scum. They literally have a license to kill. They can shoot down anyone on the street at any time and the courts will be on their side. The only people that are safe from cops are white people and other cops. They terrorize the black community and every day the president, the mayor and other fake politicians do nothing to help the people. I been living in Brooklyn for over 20+ years now and the only thing I've seen is blacks being targeted everyday by corrupted cops. I've seen cops search people's car illegally because they don't know their rights. I've seen cops gang up and beat innocent people because they didn't respond in kind to their orders. The mayor is the ring leader of the hostility between the people and the police. He protects the cops and allows them to constantly act the way they do. I'm scared sometimes to leave my home because of fear of running into the police. When I was a kid the biggest threat I had to worry about was gangs trying to harm me. Now the biggest threat I have to worry about is the police. They are a legal gang that gets away with murder every day. My taxes pay their salary.

The people are paying the cops basically to kill us. I never voted for my taxes to go to cops salaries but what do I know, I'm just a black man."

Sex: Male
Age: 19
Race: African American

"Living in this country is insane. It is like death trap design to kill black folks. The moment I got my license and I was driving my dad's Audi, and I got pulled over. Not even a day went by before the cops pulled me over trying to harass me. I was on my way home from a party and I was trying to drop my friend's home. The block I was driving down was deserted, not a car in sight. I was driving very slowly looking for my friends address when a car pulled up next to me asking me what I was doing. I asked the white men what they wanted and who they were and they said they were cops. I said I'm looking for an address and if I was doing something wrong. The police officers then told my friend to step out of the car and asked for my license. They tried searching my car but I warned them they didn't have a warrant nor my permission. I asked what I was being pulled over for and the cops said that the color of my brake light was orange instead of red. What a terrible excuse to use to pull over someone, I would have rather him just tell the truth and admit it was because I was a black kid driving a nice car. At that point I told my friend to go to the back of the car and tell me what color the light was when I hit the brake and with no surprise he told me it was red. So obviously these racist cops had one agenda, and it was to try and plant phony charges on me. After they completed their fake routine check I was free to go. My first day driving and look what it got me; two cops performing their duty of harassment. I guess this is what I have to look forward to when it comes to driving as a black man in this country."

4.

We have seen an enormous amount of African Americans in today's world become successful. Through the use of different artistic and academic outlets, Blacks represent a much larger portion of successful Americans. The media is perhaps the most Racist group of organizations working together in the United States. The majority of the news written in articles and posted on blogs sites, and shared through social media are exaggerated stories used to boost readers. Fox, CNN, The Daily News, The New York Times, and The Wall Street Journal, carry very little merit and truth in the information they feed Americans. African Americans are always portrayed in a negative aspect when referred to in the media. They are portrayed in such a negative sphere that when Whites, Police officers and other Races see African Americans all they can think of is what they see in the media. The media plays the biggest role in the formation of Race Perception.

According to the media African Americans are the most violent, ignorant, low achieving individuals in society. How can this be true if the majority of school massacres are committed by Whites, and the majority of major crimes done in this country are committed by Whites? There are over 2.5 million people being incarcerated in the United States and of that, close to 70% are

African American. Articles are written everyday about the number of African Americans serving sentences in prison, but very few articles are written detailing the crimes done by African Americans that led to them being incarcerated. Racial stereotypes are usually created by negative media portrayals. As the news and other outlets paints this image of the Black man and how dangerous he is, the media instills this image in Americans minds which fuels the fear of African Americans.

African Americans are commonly perceived as being either an athlete or musician. Unless they are applying themselves to something that involves running, jumping, or singing, Black people serve no purpose. Over the years we have seen more African Americans obtain wealth through business and academia but the perception of what African Americans are capable of has not changed. If we examine the sea of roles that are available to African American actors, we can conclude that most African Americans do not get lead roles. If the entire cast of a movie is Black, Hollywood will more than likely ensure that it is a comedy of some sort. It is as if Hollywood is not ready for Black actors to take on serious roles that relays a positive message to society. Why would they be ready for that? If Black actors are represented more in movies as educated young men and women with a higher purpose than just comedy the perception of African Americans in society would change. To White America, African Americans are entertainers. They are thrilled by Blacks aerobatic skills, their high jumping capabilities, their massive strength in sports, but letting an African American have an opinion about political, social, and economic factors that impacts everyone in this country; well to White America that would be like allowing a toddler to drive a car.

If we examine Black directors like Spike Lee who has created and directed numerous educational pieces and the difficulties he has had in Hollywood when creating serious movies, we can see that he is marginalized. Hollywood does not support Spike Lee's ventures because his movies are a depiction of African Americans and their ability to think critically. He goes beyond the common stereotypical roles that African Americans play in movies. Counter to that, Tyler Perry movies have done much better financially than Spike Lee's movies, not because they are better but because they fit the classic stereotypical roles Black actors are used to playing. Hollywood supports Tyler Perry because he creates comedy, which falls in the realm of what White America is used to seeing from African Americans.

Rap uses spoken words to express emotions. It is a young art form that was started sometime in the 1970's and carries its roots back to jazz music. Rap was created by African Americans to relay stories about life, politics, economics, social class, material achievements, as well as sex and drugs. Rappers are like reporters that relay messages to society. Rap music is depicted as one of the many causes of violence in the Black community. Crime existed before rap, so how can rap be the cause of something that was in existence before it was conceived? CNN and other news stations report death, drugs, celebrity gossip and violence every day, if an African American does the same thing on a platform that involves music, White America and the media will do their best to portray these artist as having malicious intentions towards society.

The media believes rap artist should control their music and use it as a tool for social awareness, but news networks and social media are not censoring the information relayed to the public. The media suggest that curse words, sexist misogynistic and derogatory words should be refrained from use. If rappers are like reporters they are merely relaying information about society. Instead of the media targeting the reason rap in many cases depicts anger and pain that can only be expressed through unconventional words, they target this art form because it is predominantly Black. Instead of figuring out why rappers discuss guns so often in their rhythms, or why they despise Police officers so much, the media will target the words rap artist say and condemn it, without understanding why these words are being used in the first place.

Testimonies on Media

Sex: Male
Age: 32
Race: African American

"I watch the news all the time and I have to be honest most of what I see on there I find disgusting. I mean every time I turn on the news all I see is another black guy getting arrested for some crime. I feel like the media publicize anything African Americans do. Last time I was watching the news two black men were being arrested for marijuana. I kept thinking to myself why are they plastering the faces of these two men all over the news for a drug that I've never seen kill anyone, but the wall street criminals that are stealing the American people's money will never see their day in court. I'm just so tired of the double standard America and the media holds African Americans to. I mean don't get me wrong I read the news but I know 90% of what I'm reading is biased opinions of editors. I'm also sick of these white politicians making blacks out to be a menace on the news. When Bloomberg was in office I felt like suing him every day. The propaganda he used as being the truth sent thousands of innocent people to jail."

Sex: Female
Age: 28
Race: African American

"The media portrays blacks as a danger to society. Most of the time I don't watch the news at all. I find that all I see on TV is the blues. This person dead, that person in jail, I can't really take it. Not to mention the fact that I've rarely seen any achievements of African Americans in the media. Whenever there is a school shooting in a white school the media implies that the shooting was a mistake and the media pushes the incident under the rug. When incidents occur in black neighborhoods the media fuel the fire and make it seem as if it was an incident waiting to occur. I can't stand small news companies because they will report anything just to get views. I believe the media is excellent at hiding the corrupt, racist actions of huge political figures. Just the other day I was watching the news speak about the rap legend Tupac and when they said his name, they referred to him as Tupac, rapper; convicted felon. Why did they need to add the convicted felon part to it? Then I saw another station introduce a white star that was behind bars recently but they didn't refer to him as a felon.

Sex: Male
Age: 26
Race: African American

"I cannot stand the way African Americans are being portrayed in the media. It actually makes my stomach sick the way blacks are portrayed on the news and on social media. Even the way African Americans are portrayed in movies sickens my stomach. I remember watching martin growing up and how Gina was the successful marketing executive who was married and happy, and could get any man she wanted, while Pam the dark skin woman was just an assistant and single with no man in site seeking her. Her career was on the ropes and it was very difficult for her to move up. Why is it that the show makes Pam out to be this woman that cannot achieve anything? The lighter skin girl was portrayed as success and the Darn skin woman was portrayed as failure. I hated that about the Martin show, but beyond that I loved the jokes they made. There are so many shows on major network television that portrays African Americans in this same light. Lighter the skin the more success an individual is, while darker skin characters always achieve nothing."

Sex: Male
Age: 39
Race: African Americans

"The commercials I see on television pretty much shows how racist this world is. I have seen so many business institute commercials, medical school commercials, even trade school commercials, and the one thing they all have in common is that they portray African Americans in a negative way. The instructors of all these commercials are always Caucasian or Indian in decent, and the students, the ones that need help or are trying to start their careers and always African Americans. So after seeing so many commercials where blacks are constantly in this position of needing help, I think a lot of blacks start to believe what they see in these commercials. They are represented as needing help starting their lives, always in a learning phase in life, and counter to that, whites are portrayed as the giver of knowledge and always in a position where they have the information and are educating others. Children at home start to believe that this is the case and that their race has nothing to offer. I believed that for so long growing up until I started reading about the many accomplishments African Americans contributed to American History. Television commercials are dangerous psychological tools that hinders the mental development of young minds."

Sex: Female
Age: 18
Race: African Americans

"The media creates a cage for blacks to succeed. Even television for children are racist in today's world. I was watching a show on Disney kids and what I saw I was blown away. There was a scene in the episode where one of the children couldn't understand a mathematical concept. The child being perceived as the educated one was an Indian child, and the child who was having difficulty learning the concepts was a black child. This type of view is always portrayed on television. I turned the channel after I saw that. As kids continue watching these television shows, they will subconsciously believe it without even knowing it. Movies like "CRASH" is a perfect example of the stereotypical, racist world we live in. Without voicing these concerns major networks will continue discriminating in this manner."

Uriah Brown

5.

What is the answer? What is the path that needs to be taken to lead Black America into prosperity? What steps should we embark on that will lead our children into a secure and healthy future? How can we ensure that Blacks receive equitable opportunities while Racism exists?

The first step is Education. Parents have to ensure their children are learning about themselves, their history, their culture and what they are capable of doing. Knowing American history is good, but examining the history and achievements of African Americans is essential to Black children becoming successful. Diversifying the lessons African Americans learn in their community can create new opportunities for Black children. Parents need to become educated as well. The majority of low income students are from upbringings where their parents have no formal education. This means parents have to do their part and pick up a book. Retrain your minds to adapt and combat this Racist country. Learn alongside your children and past down that knowledge to them so they can face the world with extensive preparation. Education does not stop the moment the school day ends. Create curriculums at home that allows you, the parent, to gradually inform your child of the necessary information needed to survive and excel in today's world.

Secondly, African Americans need to attack the White economy where it hurts. For decades minorities have begged and pleaded with America for fair wages, equal employment opportunities, fair housing and so much more. Each time their voices have been drowned out with Racist laws, and law enforcement officials using their weapons against them. Since this country does not want to grant Blacks the rights and freedom they deserve, they need to take it by force. Minorities need to boycott all White businesses. This is easier said than done, considering the amount of goods and services that are supplied by White businesses. If they cannot give Blacks the rights they deserve, why give them your money? Keep your money in your communities. Only shop and spend money at Black businesses. This means no longer eating at White owned restaurants, do not shop for household goods at White brand name stores, and do not buy clothing from White brand name clothing stores. Every decision concerning spending should be made taking one's own community into account. Again, I do not expect this to happen overnight, but a gradual change needs to occur if African Americans want to survive in this country. Black businesses need to make themselves known, and once Blacks are spending consistently at these businesses, it is the job of these firms to then give back to the Black community to uplift the next generation.

Boycotting the MTA and other White owned transportation services that over charge their consumers must happen now. Dr. King did it in 1955 and it can happen again today. African Americans need to stop giving money to a system that does not care whether they live or die. Getting to work and travelling is important, which is why a system needs to be created to help minorities stay mobile. All those able and capable of walking to work should do so. Substituting metro cards with bicycles will create a financial crisis for the MTA while aiding with health concerns for African Americans. Black people spend almost 5 times more than any other Race in this country, yet they manage to accumulate less assets than everyone. Think of the results that could be achieved if that money was staying in the Black community.

Closing all accounts with White owned banks is critical to this turnaround succeeding. Moving funds to Black banks such as Carvers bank, First State bank, and commonwealth National bank are necessary to Black America's success. These banks have to play their part in ensuring consumers are receiving equitable results by banking with their institution. Giving customers incentives to join through higher interest rates on saving accounts is critical to this plan working.

Thirdly, African Americans need to do the opposite of everyone else. They need to break the addiction of spending. It is a powerful addiction that fuels the White economy and keeps the Black economy poor. The moment minorities get their pay checks, they give it right back to the firms that are the architects of their economic stall. To create real economic change takes changes in personal behavior. Consumer spending accounts for nearly 70% of Gross Domestic Product. By controlling their spending habits, African Americans can dictate where best they believe their money should be going.

Fourthly, Black people need to become Homeowners. Homeownership is the platform used by so many to demand control and authority in America. By owning property African Americans can gain access to rental income and turn their properties into businesses. Consumers give away almost half their annual salaries on rental expenses without ever owning the space they are renting. Through homeownership that same spending will go towards creating equity.

Lastly, Life insurance is crucial in creating and sustaining wealth. It guarantees payment to the beneficiary of the policy. For years White Americans have ensured their children's future by leaving them hundreds of thousands of dollars in Life Insurance money. This money in many cases can be used to start a new business, place down payments on homes, pay off debt, renovate existing homes to increase the property value, and even pay for funeral arrangements. Life Insurance guarantees that children are taken care of regardless of their financial situation. Minorities must ensure they draft the right policy that will enable their family's total assets to grow over generations.

This book is intended to be used as a tool to inform White America of the harsh conditions African Americans and other minority groups have to live through. It is a unique lens developed to access the daily conditions ascribed to Blacks. Maybe after reading "The Black Bubble", America will understand the trials & hardships African Americans face in this country.

<u>References</u>

- Talbert, Marcia Wade, and Robin White Goode. "Black Americans Education Crisis." Black Enterprise 42.2(2011):71-75.academic search com,plete.web.27 May 2012.

- Noguera, Pedro A."Saving Black And Latino Boys".Phi Delta Kaplan 93.5 (2012):8-12. Academic Search Complete.web.27 May 2012.

- Baumgartner,Lisa M., Juanita Johnson-Bailey. "Racism and White privilege in adult education graduate programs: Admissions, retentions, and curricula". New direction for adult & continuing education125 (2010):27-40.academic search complete.web.28 May 2012.

- Robert M. Sellers,etal."say it loud—I'm black and I'm proud":parents' messages about race, racial discrimination, And academic achievement in African American Boys."Journal of negro education 78.3(2009):246-259. Academic search complete.web.27 May 2012.

- Rothstein, Richard."why are our schools segregated."Educational Leadership.May2013,Vol.70 Issue 8,p50-55.6p.Aceademic search complete.

- Cobb-Roberts, Deirdre, and vonzell Agosto. "Underrepresented women in higher education:An overview." Negro education review 62/63.1-4 (2011):7-11. Academic search complete. Web. 28 may 2012

- Mazama, Ama, and Garvey Lundy. " African American Homeschooling As Racial Protectionism." Journal Of Black Studies 43.7 (2012):723-748.

- Rozansky-Lloyd, Carol. "African Americans In Schools: Tiptoeing Around Racism." Western Journal Of Black Studies 29.3(2005): 595-604. Academic Search Complete. Web.12 June 2013.

- Wright, Scott W.,"New York Mayor Declares War on CUNY."Community College week.02/09/98,Vol.10 issue 14, p2. 1/5p.Academic Search Premier.

- Wright, Scott W.,"This isn't working."Black Issues in Higher Education.02/19/98,Vol.14issue 26, p14. 2p. 3 Black and White Photographs.Academic Search Premier.

- UCLA School of Public Affairs Critical race Studies.http://spacrs.wordpress.com/what-is-critical-race-theory/

- Nussbaumer, John. "MISUSE OF THE LAW SCHOOL ADMISSIONS TEST, RACIAL DISCRIMINATION, AND THE DE FACTO QUOTA SYSTEM FOR RESTRICTING AFRICAN-AMERICAN ACCESS TO THE LEGAL PROFESSION."St. John's Law Review. Winter2006, Vol. 80 Issue 1, p167-181-F. 21p.Academic Search Premier

- http://www.thecrimson.com/article/1998/10/2/report-shows-lsat-score-gap-pa/

- Pager, Devah, and Hana Shephred. "The Sociology Of Discrimination: Racial Discrimination In Employment, Housing, Credit and Consumer Markets." Annual Review Of Sociology 34.1(2008): 181-209. Academic Search Complete.web.17 June 2013.

- Wilson, George. "Race And Job Dismissal: African American/White Differences In Their Sources During The Early Work Career." American Behavioral Scientist48.9 (2005): 1182-1199. Academic Search Complete. Web. 17 June 2013

- Noe, Hollenbeck, Gerhart, wright. Fundamentals of Human resource Management. New York: McGraw Hill/Irwin, 2011.

- Rockwell, Paul. "Fighting The Fires Of racism." Nation249.20(1989): 714-718. Academic Search Complete.Web. 17 June 2013

- Pathology of the white privileged. Tim Wise. Youtube.2007

- Khosrovani, Masoomeh, and James W. Ward. "African Americans perception Of Access To Workplace Opportunities: A survey Of employees in Houston Texas." Journal Of Cultural Diversity 18.4(2011):134-141.Academic Search Complete.Web13 Jan. 2014.

- http://cnsnews.com/news/article/michael-w-chapman/unemployment-rate-down-05-56-months-obama-became-president

- http://www.politifact.com/truth-o-meter/statements/2012/oct/17/barack-obama/barack-obama-says-his-administration-has-created-5/

- http://www.youtube.com/watch?v=rfJHx0Gj6ys

- http://www.policemisconduct.net/2010-npmsrp-police-misconduct-statistical-report/

- Chaney,Cassandra , and Ray Robertson."Racism and Police Brutality In America."Journal of American Studies 17.4(2013):480-505.Academic search complete.Web.30 Mar.2014.
- http://www.latimes.com/local/cityhall/la-me-crime-stats-20151015-story.html

Glossary

Affirmative action- A policy that was created to protect under-represented minority groups. The policy takes factors such as an individual's race, religion, and sex into account when representing them in employment and business.

Critical Race Theory- An academic term used to examine society, culture, race, law, and power. This theory analyzes Racism and recognizes that it is implanted in the roots of our society. It is used to analyze the structure of society and ensures that this structure is based on White Privilege and White Supremacy.

Human capital- The skills, knowledge and capabilities of the human resources that helps to produce goods and services for a firm.

Meritocracy- A philosophy that believes individuals advance in society based on demonstrated achievements and intellectual superiority.

Racial Socialization- The process by which parents teach their children about the significance and meaning of race.

Racism- A system of disadvantage based on race.

The Black Bubble- An institutionalized barrier that creates a barricade to success.

White Privilege- An advantage White Americans possess that gives them more opportunities than minorities.

ABOUT THE AUTHOR

The youngest of four boys, Uriah Brown holds a BBA degree in International Business and a Masters of Science in Business Administration from Brooklyn College. At 23 Mr. Brown became a College Professor teaching courses in Economics and Business at the Long Island Business Institute and The Professional Business College of New York City. Uriah's passion for Civil & Human Rights grew as he got older. Witnessing constant Racial injustice gave Uriah the confidence to write "The Black Bubble". He was born in Brooklyn, New York and studied Asian cultures while traveling overseas to China. This is Uriah's first book and his goal is to critically analyze what issues impact African Americans on a daily basis and to create a solution that will enable Black America to thrive in this racist economy.

Use the blank pages and discuss whether you agree or disagree with the points laid out in "The Black Bubble." Critically analyze the arguments and decide whether a solution can be found. Use the pages to create a blueprint on what you think African Americans best approach to socioeconomic justice may be.

6.

Notes

Notes

Uriah Brown

Notes

Notes

Notes

Notes

Uriah Brown

Notes

Notes

Notes

Notes

Notes

Notes

Notes

Notes

Notes

Notes

Notes

Notes

Uriah Brown

Notes

Made in the USA
Middletown, DE
28 February 2016